Grow U

How To Ac

Shoshi Katis

Table of Contents

Introduction

How do I get a job?

How do I pay taxes?

How do I rent a place to live?

How do I pay bills?

What is credit? How do I get it?

Everybody wants to be a financially fit, responsible grown up, but how? Managing your own money is the best way to own your life and feed your goals. You want to be independent and make your own rules? The only way to do that is pay your own bills and live within your means. There are some hard and fast rules to the financial world and some big no-no's when it comes to your status. It's easy enough to learn, and it is to your complete benefit. Life isn't easy or fair, but we should all have the basic skills to be in control of our lives, and that requires more than brief instructions on how to balance your checking account.

Chapter 1: The First 18 Years

Home is where you come from, it's part of who you are, who you will become. Your family, friends, teachers,they all have a part in shaping you. In a perfect world all children should grow up with equal measures of love, kindness, encouragement, and friendships to see us into healthy adults. Unfortunately, this is not the norm. Families are broken, abuse in many forms is common, school systems fail, and people are generally not very nice to each other.

In the years you live at home, your focus should be on school, friends, driving and discovering how you fit in to this big world. Sometimes, events at home and school make it hard to focus on learning. Imagine kids who have goals and dreams and skills that are not encouraged, or worse, they are discouraged. No guidance with getting a drivers license or a job. Some of us are promised to be on our own with no support after graduation.

Everyone has different circumstances and different choices to make. No matter what hand you have been dealt in this life, you are not yet who you will become. It will take time, and it will not be easy, but you can do anything that you want. Some people will have it easier than you... and some people will have it much harder. We weren't all created equal after all, but we all deserve to have a good life. Try to be kind and look out for each other.

While you are a minor, you cannot be legally bound to a contract without a parent or guardian co signature. Even if you have it tough at home, you can't legally work, rent a place, have a bank account, etc until you are 18, without your parents help. You have nothing but time, so you may as well spend it masterminding your own future.

Chapter 2: Career Path

Part of what makes it so difficult to choose a career path to follow is that we are made to feel that it is the most important decision of our life and if we choose wrong... that's it, game over, you lose. It is important, but there is a bigger picture here for you to understand.

School is a system, kids don't always recognize that it is there to benefit them. You have to know how to use it. Here's the thing... if you graduate from high school with no job skills you will be severely limited as to the jobs you are qualified for. There are only two logical options. You either attend a vo-tech program in high school, or you go to college, because you need job skills!

You are likely to need to go back to school every time you change your career, and that is fine. The big deal about being in high school is that it is free. It's important that you don't waste that. Even if you are undecided, pick something, train for a job. You can always go back for something else later. In the meantime, you will be trained and able to work.

Some high schools now offer dual enrollment with local colleges, meaning you could possible graduate from high school with a college degree, for free! YES, Do that! Especially if you are undecided on what career path to choose. College is the best place to be when you are looking for direction. You will be among people of all ages and ideas.

Indeed, education is like leveling up in the game of life. You can never waste your time educating yourself. Do you really think you will ever know all that you need to know? As long as you follow school rules, you have a right to earn that high school diploma. Don't ever let anyone steal that from you. If you quit, you will be missing out on the free education and the opportunities to learn a trade or skill that will qualify you for a job.

Quit School = You may be hired for some minimum wage positions. You must pay to level up and get your GED/High School Equivalent, which you could have received for free.

GED = You are qualified for some minimum wage jobs. You must pay to level up and get into a program that you would have received for free as a student.

High School = You are qualified to participate in programs of interest for free. This is the time and place where you will have the most opportunities and resources for leveling up.

Vo-Tech = You are trained and qualified with skills to enter a specific field of work. If you decide you'd like to try a different field. You just have to save, budget, and go back to school.

College = You never lose your credit or degree, but you can add to it, indefinitely. It's never a bad time, never too late to go back to school and educate yourself...Level up!

A note about student loans: Why would you put yourself so far in debt before you've started working and living? It could take years to pay off that loan. How will you pay that off later while trying to also live and pay bills and provide for yourself and possibly a family in the future. If you have trouble paying this loan, it could ruin your credit. It's interesting that the only loan you can get at 18 is a student loan. It's too easy, too good to be true. Where there is a will, there is another way, I promise. Your first adult decision should probably not be to sign up for debt. If you don't think you can work your way through college now, how on earth will you be able to pay for it later? Remember too, that low credit scores mean you will pay higher deposits for utility bills, higher interest rates on purchases,etc.

Chapter 3: Drivers License

A drivers license is usually the first big milestone for us. Our first taste of freedom. How quickly we learn the cost of that freedom. Most of us make it our business to know our state laws about how and when we get the privilege to drive, (if not I'd refer you to your state DMV website to find out).

In most cases, you must get a permit/provisional license for a required time period before getting your drivers license. Aside from driving, your license will serve as you photo ID. You need this even if you never plan on driving. You could get a state issued photo ID instead, but that is what people use when they can't get a drivers license. It's a written and then a driving test to get your license. Unless you abuse your privileges, you don't have to take another driving class or test again. You will renew every 5 years by going in to the DMV taking an eye test, a new picture, and paying the fee. If your name or address changes you will also have to notify the DMV.

Before you buy a car, there are many things to consider. You have to add the cost of tax, tags, and title to the total of the sale. You must have insurance on the car before you drive away in it. You will need routine maintenance. A good mechanic can change your oil and diagnose any issues. He will guide you on what your next maintenance routine will be, and tell you ahead of time when parts may need replacing and how much that will be.

When you purchase a car with cash, you need the title signed by the owner and yourself. You'll sign a liability waiver releasing the previous owner from all responsibility. You go to the DMV get a new title, tag, and registration. Don't forget that right before purchasing the vehicle you want to get insurance so you are covered, you can't get tags or registration without it. You can get limited liability insurance (the cheapest), but as a new driver insurance can be costly.

If you decide to take out an automobile loan, you must carry full coverage insurance until the loan is paid off, that's the law. With an auto loan, the dealership likely adds on the expenses of tax, tag, title, interest,and a few more fees. Be very careful when signing a contract for a loan. Salesmen have a way of selling products or extended warranty packages that cost thousands of dollars. Carefully, look over the contract and the final cost before signing. Don't be afraid to walk away from a deal that doesn't work for you. No matter what happens to the car or your job, you are still responsible for paying off the loan.

When selling a car or canceling insurance on your car, you must turn in your tags to the DMV, (unless you register them to another insured vehicle) or you will be fined, and your drivers license could be suspended.

The last thing I'd like to say about driving is, be prepared for the worst. Keep supplies in your car to keep you warm and dry in case of being stranded in bad weather. A handy list of what to do in case of an accident will keep you from being overwhelmed if it happens. Don't leave the scene, take pictures, exchange drivers license and insurance information. If there is significant damage, injury, or death... call the police.

Don't get too upset, try to keep calm. Accidents happen, that's why we have insurance. It matters most that everyone is alright.

Chapter 4: Set Your Goals

Everybody alive has had hopes and dreams, and some have even achieved them. There is a big difference between those who succeed and those who simply dream of success. To realize your dreams you must set goals and come up with a plan of action. They can be all the things you want, and none of the things you don't, it's your list. Listing them is going to be the easiest part of reaching your goals, but also, the most essential. Throughout your life it is important to update and change your list, as you will surely grow and change as a person. Without taking time to reflect on your life and goals periodically, you will become a victim of life and circumstances. You must keep focus on your path or you will wander aimlessly with inadequate results.

Long Term Goals

Obviously there are things you want that will take time and money. List them as long term goals, and don't leave anything out. This is your life you can have and do anything, dream big. If you don't have them listed you will always see them as a distant idea. A good range of time for the long term is five years. Where do you see yourself in five years? Where do you want to be? What do you want to be doing? You can make it happen! In fact, you are the only one who can make your dreams come true. Try to list at least three long term goals and remember to always reflect on your life, keeping your list current and focusing on what is important to you.

Short Term Goals

Your short term goals are the things you can do now that will help you progress closer to your long term goals. Some of them may be for immediate survival that have nothing to do with the long term. Don't let yourself get too comfortable in the day to day life that you neglect your future dreams, though. The future will be shaped by you and your actions. It won't just manifest simply because you desire it, you have to keep your focus.

Perhaps you want to own a restaurant one day. What actions can you take now to help you achieve this later? You could start working in a restaurant as a hostess, bus-person, cook, or server. You could work your way up to management. These are all actions that will benefit you and introduce you to people and opportunities geared in the direction you are going.

If you can't define your goals and have no plan of action for your life, then you are not in control and you are at the mercy of all that is unfair and hard in this world. You could end up settling for much less than you intended. Fortunately, opportunities of convenience happen when we most need it. A job offer when you are out of money is a blessing, for sure. But, these are not permanent destinations, so much as, temporary shelters. Don't ever lose sight of your dreams.

Work and save to reach these goals. They will change as you either achieve your goals or change your desires. It's alright as long as you are the one making the decisions. If you want to be successful in life, then you must assert your own ideas and actions. I have read myself that successful people get up thirty minutes earlier than they have to just to have time devoted to their own thoughts. They record them, and mostly they are just ramblings... but once in a while they have that million dollar idea. We all have it in us, we just need to allow ourselves time to reflect.

The truth is, we have nothing but time. We are going to live until we die, and since we don't know when that will be, there is no hurry. You can be a teacher and then change your mind and be a real estate agent, Your time wasn't wasted as long as you did it for yourself. You can be a waitress and decide to become an accountant. You can do anything you want, and then... you can change your mind at anytime and do something different. You really are only limited by your own imagination. Well, that and money, but we'll get to that.

Right now make a list for your short and long term goals. It's alright if they change, we are humans and we grow and change all the time. Maintain your lists and keep them current. This is your life and it should be your pleasure and your priority to be the master of it.

Example:

Long Term Goals	Short Term Goals
LPN Job	Maintain GPA to qualify for LPN program
LPN to RN Program	Talk to guidance counselor and program director about scholarships.
RN Job	Save for your RN program in case scholarships don't cover the total cost.
Camaro	Save $26,000 for Camaro. You could save half for a down payment and finance the rest.
Home with 50+ acres	Save about $75,000 for a down payment on home.
Helicopter	Get a license to fly helicopter. Save $100,000 more or less.

Chapter 5: Income

Income is the money you earn on a regular schedule that will dictate your afford-abilities. As you work and throughout your years you will create a work record, and it amounts to experience and references. No matter what job or career you choose always do your best. Show up, be on time, and be professional. It will easily set you apart from those who take no pride in their work. You need a consistent income for many reasons, most important, the money itself. If you desire to be independent you must have an income. When you are really down on your luck you can sell anything you might have of value. However that isn't a stable income. A job does not define you but it does pay you.

Employment

Looking for a job is the hardest job there is. You can scan the job searches, or you can look up a specific company and see what they offer via their career link. Many times the best way to find a job is through word of mouth. Tell people you know that you are looking for work. Chances are someone you know will know someone who needs help, and since they know you personally they can also be a reference. Unless you are just coming into the workforce you need work references to be considered for jobs. When you apply for a job you need a credible work history. It's OK to change jobs, but you shouldn't be without work in-between.

Each job will be a reference for the next. In order to keep a good work record with good references, be a good employee. Be dependable, be on time, do your job, help others. When you are ready to leave a job, make sure you give notice. Two weeks is standard notice. When you find a new job they will appreciate and understand that you have to finish out your previous commitment. Not only do you need good references, you also will need to explain any gaps of time in between jobs. It is typically expected that you work steady with no time off between jobs. If you quit without notice, you will have an unusable bad reference and an inconsistency in your work history. Try never to quit a job until you have another job in place.

When you interview, dress professionally, and ask questions. You want to make a good impression and show that you will be an asset to the company, but you also want to know all that the company has to offer you. What will your schedule be? How much will you make? Will you be eligible for health benefits? Paid vacations? Yearly raises? Etc. When applying for your first job, you may not be eligible for many positions or benefits. The first couple of jobs you work will be for the experience, not necessarily because you wanted those positions.

Pay day is different for every place you work. Most common is weekly or bi-weekly, and they usually hold your first check Let's say, you will get paid every Friday and you started on Monday (the beginning of the pay period). You will not get a pay check this Friday, it will be held until the next. You will get all of your money owed, it just comes one week behind. This also means that when you quit , you will have one week of pay still coming to you.

Most employers offer direct deposit of your paychecks into your bank account. They will need your banks routing number as well as the account number that you would like your deposits made. These numbers are on the bottom of your bank checks.

Once you've established an income, you are on your way to

independence. It feels great to earn money and decide what you will spend it on. You will learn that it dwindles away quickly and you'll be thankful that another check is coming. Keep a record of your paychecks and the taxes you pay. I use to file my pay stubs, but now going paperless, I can view all my pay stubs on line. Make sure they are correct as people and computers make mistakes all the time.

Throughout your life, be a decent human being. Be kind, respectful, and generous... what you put out there always returns to you. When you are brand new in the work force you don't have a work history or experience. This is why you hear people say, "It's not always what you know, but who you know." If you don't know anybody and have no skills, you start at the beginning, food service, retail stores, laborer, etc. Remember, you won't start off with the job of your dreams, but you will get experience and a good reference.

A long time ago, you used to go into a business and ask if they were hiring and fill out an application. If they didn't call within a few days, you would call them to show you are interested in employment. They would then call you in for an interview and a day or so later you would get a call with a job offer. I suppose some employers still do this, but most applications are on line now. If you have applied for jobs and not received any calls yet, you can call them after a few days to express interest in employment. Don't worry, soon you will be working, and then, forevermore.

Chapter 6: Taxes

You will have to pay taxes on all the money you earn. Most employers will have you fill out W4 tax forms when you start working. They will take taxes out of your income based on the information you give them. If you are a teenager living with your parents, they likely claim you as a dependent. That means on your tax forms you would claim zero. However, if you are on your own and no one can claim you, (they would need your social security number to claim you) then you have two options.

You can still claim zero, and the maximum amount of taxes will be taken out of your paychecks. At tax time, you would then claim one dependent, (yourself) and you will get a refund.

The other option is to claim 1 (yourself) all year and have less taxes taken out of your paychecks. At the end of the year you may owe a little, or you may get a small refund. It's up to you, which way you do it, it matters very little because you will pay your taxes ,either way.

I am not a tax expert, I'm simply telling you something that we all have to learn on our own because nobody ever mentions this. Tax papers can confuse anyone, especially a kid applying for their first job. I personally claim zero all year then claim myself at tax time, and I always get a refund. Also, if you are eligible to fill out the 1040EZ form at tax time, just do it yourself. It is very easy and comes with instructions. Don't pay anyone to do your taxes until they become too complicated to do on your own. When you own land, home, or business, and have dependents then you may need a professional accountant.

Sometimes you may be employed as a contractor and that means you will have to pay your own taxes as they are not taken out of your income. You will receive a 1099 at the end of the year for the amount you were payed, and you will owe taxes on it. If you have a job like this try to save 20% of your income from each pay check to pay your taxes at the end of the year.

Chapter 7: Checking Account

If you haven't already, the next step to establishing your financial status is opening a checking account to deposit your steady paychecks. There are three very important forms of ID you will need to do most everything. These are Birth Certificate, Social Security Card, and Drivers License. You will need two of these to open a bank account.

Choose A Bank

Banks are a business, and they all offer different benefits. You could spend plenty of time researching your specific needs. However, you may not have any particular needs other than to have an account at first. In this case, you could ask your friends or relatives where they bank. You could just go in to a local bank that has been around your town since you can remember. It's wise to choose a bank that is close to you, or has the most branches in your area of travels. Convenience is key, you want to have access to your money whenever you want.

What Kind Of Account

To start, a simple free checking account is ideal. You don't want to have to pay bank fees. Usually, they require that you direct deposit your pay check or that you maintain a specific balance at all times. Whatever they require find out before you open an account. It can cause major headaches for you if you bounce a check or run out of money because your bank charged you fees. Banks make good money off of irresponsible habits. You can't cheat the bank or move your business elsewhere once you accumulate fees to avoid paying them. If you have a negative balance they will take the fees from your next deposit leaving you short on funds, again.

What To Know

It is not necessary to purchase checks unless you know that you will be using them. You will get a debit card to handle transactions, and most bills can be paid on line. It is important to know your banks routing number as well as your checking account number. If your employer offers direct deposit they will need this information. This is your main account and your deposits and spending habits are being recorded and judged.

If you put $500 in you account and you spend $22.33 in gas and $34.17 on dinner then you only have $443.50 left. You should keep a register or a small note pad with your balance and all the transactions you've made. It will show you what you spend your money on.

You start with your balance. Each line you add is either a deposit or debit. You need the date, who the money went to, and how much. Either add the deposit to your balance, or subtract if it was a debit. You should never be unaware of how much money you have, that's how money disappears, unnoticed.

Chapter 8: Savings Account

Ideally, when you have at least $100 saved you should put that into a savings account. Just revisit your bank and take your two forms of ID. Having a checking and savings account shows that you can manage your money. Your deposits and spending habits are recorded and judged and you want to keep that record clean and smooth so that you can begin to establish credit.

Save Money

Some banks offer simple plans that allow you to contribute to your savings even when you don't think you have money to do so. For instance, when you use your debit card for say $10.50, you would actually deduct $11.00 (rounded up to the nearest $1) from your checking and the extra change ($.50) would be deposited into your savings. It adds up quickly. My bank offers a similar plan. Each time I use my debit card, my total is rounded up $1. That means if I spend $10.50 in gas on my debit card, I would actually deduct $11.50 from my checking account and put $1 into my savings. I save over $500 a year with that method alone.

If your bank doesn't have special offers like that, you can simply apply that logic to your own transactions and at the end of the week or month transfer that money from one account to the other yourself.

Some investors say you should be saving at least 10% of your income. If you make $400 a week then $40 should go into your savings account. This is difficult to do when cost of living is not in proportion with your living wages. Set a goal that is realistic for you and stick to it like your future depends on it, because it does. If you have an income and are barely scraping by, then $5 a week will not kill you but in a year it will amount to a savings of $260. In five years it will grow to $1300.

You would be wise to make scheduled savings deposits, either weekly, or monthly. Regular deposits show good money management. Committing to a minimal amount of say, $25 every other Friday, (and you can always deposit extra) looks better to creditors than making inconsistent deposits of random amounts.

You should try to save six months salary to cover your cost of living in case you are out of work for a period of time. After reaching that amount, begin saving for a new goal. Save 5% of your income for investing, and learn about investing

Chapter 9: Credit

Warning! Alert! Proceed with Caution!

It's really easy so don't make it complicated. You have already been told the horror stories of how credit can and has turned lives upside down. Credit is a system of scores and if you don't know the rules you will score poorly and end up head over heels in debt. That score follows you deeper and farther than you are aware.

Who checks your credit score? Some employers, landlords, public utilities (electricity, water, cable), insurance, creditors that work with automobile loans, and mortgages. You will see why that matters in each instance as you read further.

To establish credit you need a stable job as well as checking and savings accounts. This is how you prove you are financially responsible and that you can in fact afford to pay for a debt. You could go directly to your bank (after 6 months to 1 year of good business) and see if you can qualify for a credit card. If not, they can tell you why and what you can do to become qualified.

Once you have a credit card there are a lot of complicated figures that add to the equation. Basically, those figures detail all the ways you will be screwed if you don't pay your balance every month. You want to use your credit card for only things that you have the money to pay for and pay that credit card off every month. If you don't you will pay interest and that adds up every month. That's how people fall into the credit card trap. Never borrow more than you can pay cash for. Credit is just a tool to earn a score, don't be fooled into treating it like extra cash. To establish credit, it is simple, Use credit, pay debt in full, repeat to earn and maintain a good score. Mission accomplished.

Do not use credit to buy things you can't pay for, Do not pay only the minimum payment on this debt and let the interest cause your bill to grow out of control. Unless you want to be rejected or pay extra money for deposits on utility bills, higher interest rates on loans, etc... Just use credit for the tool that it is.

There are few occasions where you will have to borrow more money than you have in cash. The first is usually an automobile, and then the (much bigger) home loan. You need good credit to purchase a home, but you can get a vehicle (at a super high interest rate) with low or no credit. It will cost you thousands in interest! Get your credit together before taking out a loan. There are other ways to get a good running vehicle until you have either the cash or credit (to save thousands less in fees and interest).

Again, Credit is a tool to establish how responsible and trustworthy you are at managing your money and debts. If you put $50 every month on your credit card to fill your motorcycle up with gas, and pay the $50 balance in full at the end of the month, for a whole year, you will raise your credit score. Pay your rent/mortgage, utility bills, etc on time! If you are late on any payments, it will count against you. Miss your car payments, the bank will repossess your car and you will still have to pay that loan off.

When you have no credit or a low score you will be financially burdened. When you get your own place and want to turn the electricity on in your name, you will pay a deposit based on your credit rating. The deposit will be $20 for some of us, for others it could be as much as $400 (or more). The same thing will happen when you call to turn the water on in your name, the cable/internet, etc. When you purchase a car it could be a difference of thousands of dollars more you could pay in interest depending on your credit score. For a home, perhaps, $100,000.00 or more over a 30 year period. Your credit score is a pretty big deal that affects so many aspects of our daily lives.

Chapter 10: Budgeting

A good budget will help you achieve your financial goals. You want to make more than you spend. You also want to have enough to save to reach your goals in a timely manner, and have a little extra money for yourself. Live within your means. If you can't afford the things you want, you have to earn more money. Hopefully, you have a job before you have any bills then you will have an easier time knowing what you can afford.

I'll give you an example of a monthly budget. You can take this formula and apply your own income and bills.

In the example, you see four weekly pay checks of $700 for one month totaling $2800. If you look under the columns for each paycheck, I broke down all the bills weekly. In the far right column is the total monthly cost of each bill listed. At the bottom is what is left over every week after paying the bills. Saving $800 a month will add up to $9600 a year, WOW!

Example:

Pay Checks	Week 1	Week 2	Week 3	Week 4	Monthly Total
	$700	$700	$700	$700	$2800

	Week 1	Week 2	Week 3	Week 4	Monthly Total
-Rent	150	150	150	150	600
-Electric	25		25	25	100
Water	10	10	10	10	40
Cable /Internet	20	20	20	20	80
Cell Phone	20	20	20	20	80
Car/Ins	115	115	115	115	460
Groc	60	60	60	60	240
Gas	20	20	20	20	80
Savings	200	200	200	200	800
Totals	$620.00	$620.00	$620.00	$620.00	$2,480.00

	Week 1	Week 2	Week 3	Week 4	Monthly Total
After paying all the bills this is what is left for you.	$80.00	$80.00	$80.00	$80.00	$320.00

If you are still at home and have very few bills (or none), you should be banking all your income. Very soon, and forevermore, you will be paying for everything. When you do have rent and utility bills, you want to be able to cover them with no more than half of your income. After saving (hopefully) 20% of your income, you will have money for the daily living expenses like groceries and gas.

When you are ready to move into your own place for the first time, it will be challenging because you are young and have no references from past rentals. You will pay for a background check and credit check. It is standard practice to sign a one year lease, and pay first and last months rent, plus a security deposit. If your rent is $800 then it will cost $2400 to move in.

The security deposit will be returned at the end of your lease if you leave the place in the same shape you found it. You will pay for damages, or trash left behind, even if it is more than the security deposit. You will want to call the electric, water, cable, and internet companies about 2-3 days before you move in to turn on the utilities in your name. As mentioned before, based on your credit score and history of bill paying, you will be required to pay a deposit to these companies. It will be credited to your account at the end of the year, and has nothing to do with the actual bill for services. When you move locally, you can transfer your services from one place to another. A longer distance move requires you to call and cancel your services 2-3 days before you want it cut off.

Estimating that it will take $3000 just to move in to your own place and $1200 monthly for a year, a budget can help figure out how to afford this. You make $1600 -$1200=$400. Don't forget groceries and cell phone. That leaves you $100 a month before savings or miscellaneous cash. You may want to find a cheaper place to rent, or find a way to increase your income.

Chapter 11: Loans and Debt

Unless it is important to my survival, I never borrow money or incur any debt. Your goal is to grow your money to save for the future. If you owe debts, then you will be working to pay that off as well as trying to survive in the present. You will not have room to save when you are in the negative.

It costs money to borrow money. You will have to take a loan out for big purchases such as, vehicles, equipment, machinery, home, land, etc. You will have to establish credit to be considered for some purchases, but you will pay thousands in interest with low or no credit score. It's best to save and build credit. After building your credit (and the income to afford it) then you can borrow money for your a home with better interest rates.

The same thing applies to student loans. Don't be fooled. Just because they are willing to loan you a pretty substantial amount of money, doesn't mean you have any business borrowing it. If you aren't stable and secure enough to pay those loan payments right now, then do not borrow the money.

Borrow = Pay extra to borrow money you already don't have yet

Save =Earn the money you need, save the extra you would have spent in interest for new tires on your Camaro.

Chapter 12: Lock Box

A secure fire and flood safe lock box is a good place to keep all of your most important valuables. This is where you might keep your birth certificate, social security card, immunization records, passport, cash, and jewelry can also be kept in a lock box. It's important to protect some things and have them handy as needed.

You should keep a separate file box, cabinet, or system or some sort as you will acquire papers that need to be kept. You should keep a file for your annual tax returns, receipts for major purchases, marriage license, mortgage, investments,and any legal documents. Most of your records you will keep indefinitely.

A lock box is a great gift idea for ages 16 and up. Birthday, Christmas, or Graduation is the perfect time as coming of age marks the way of becoming more responsible. I hope this book has helped you to understand how you can live well and within your own means. If so I hope you will leave a review, and maybe, suggest or purchase it for someone else who may enjoy it.

About the Author

Shoshi Katis is a certified phlebotomist and mother of two. She is an avid reader and writer and this is her very first published book.

Always be kind, it matters!

Other Books by this Author

None yet, this is my first book. More to come!

Printed in Great Britain
by Amazon